K. CONNORS

ASVAB Exam Study Guide 2025

Your Comprehensive Guide to Mastering the Armed Services Vocational Aptitude Battery

First edition

This book was professionally typeset on Reedsy.
Find out more at reedsy.com

Contents

Introduction: Understanding the ASVAB Exam and Your Path to Success

So, you've decided to take the ASVAB. Maybe you're excited. Maybe you're terrified. Maybe you're holding this book because someone shoved it into your hands and said, *"Trust me, you'll need this."* Either way, welcome. You're in the right place, and we're going to tackle this beast together.

The ASVAB, or Armed Services Vocational Aptitude Battery (say that five times fast), is more than just a test. It's a gateway, a key, and - depending on how you approach it - a giant, looming monster or a pretty manageable hill to climb. But let's get one thing straight: this exam isn't about tricking you or proving how much random trivia you've memorized. It's about measuring your strengths and figuring out where you might excel in the military - or even in civilian careers. In short, it's kind of a big deal.

Now, let's clear up a misconception: The ASVAB isn't just one test. It's a collection of subtests, each one assessing a different skill set. Arithmetic reasoning? Check. Mechanical comprehension? Yep. Word knowledge, general science, assembling objects - it's like a buffet of academic and practical skills. Some sections might feel like they're custom-made for you, while others might make you want to throw this book across the room. That's normal.

But before we dive into strategies and tips, let's take a step back and talk about *why* this matters. Whether you're gunning for a specific military role, hoping for a high score to access better opportunities, or just trying to get through it without a complete meltdown, understanding the purpose behind the ASVAB can make all the difference.

Why the ASVAB Matters

The ASVAB isn't just about getting into the military. Sure, it's a requirement for enlistment, but your score can shape your entire military career. A high score doesn't just open doors - it kicks them wide open. Better roles, specialized training, and sometimes even enlistment bonuses are all tied to how well you perform on this exam.

On the flip side, if the military isn't your long-term plan, guess what? Your ASVAB score can still help you. The skills and aptitudes measured on this test are relevant in a ton of civilian jobs, especially in technical and mechanical fields. So even if you're not 100% sure where life is taking you, doing well on this test is a solid investment in *you.*

And let's be real: tests have a bad rap. They're stressful, they can feel arbitrary, and they have a way of reducing complex humans into cold, hard numbers. But the ASVAB isn't trying to judge your worth. It's trying to understand your potential.

How to Approach This Guide

This book isn't magic - it won't make you an ASVAB genius overnight. But it *will* give you the tools, strategies, and practice you need to walk into that testing room with confidence. We'll break down each section of the test, explain what you need to know, and throw in some practice questions so you can flex those brain muscles.

But - and this is important - don't just *read* this book. Use it. Highlight stuff. Scribble in the margins. Dog-ear pages. Make it yours. Studying isn't passive; it's an active, sweaty, slightly frustrating process. Embrace it.

You'll also notice that this guide doesn't talk down to you. There's no academic snootiness here, no ivory-tower lecturing. Just real talk, clear explanations, and a little bit of humor to keep things from getting too dry.

The Big Picture

The ASVAB isn't forever. It's a few hours of your life that can set you up for years of opportunities. So while it's important to take it seriously, don't let it consume you. This isn't an unscalable mountain - it's just a test. And like any test, it's conquerable with preparation, patience, and maybe a little caffeine.

So, take a deep breath. Crack your knuckles. And let's get started.

By the time you finish this book, you'll know more about arithmetic reasoning, mechanical comprehension, and paragraph understanding than you ever thought possible. And hey, you might even enjoy parts of it. Stranger things have happened.

Let's do this.

Chapter 1: ASVAB Basics – What You Need to Know

Alright, let's cut straight to the chase. You've got this massive test looming over you, and it feels like someone just handed you a map written in a foreign language. The ASVAB isn't just any old standardized test - it's the gatekeeper to your military future, and, honestly, it's a pretty big deal. But before we dive into strategies, practice questions, and tips that'll make your brain sweat, we need to start with the basics.

First off, what *is* the ASVAB? The Armed Services Vocational Aptitude Battery isn't just a test; it's a multi-aptitude assessment designed to figure out what you're naturally good at. Are you a math whiz? Do you have a knack for mechanics? Can you decipher complex paragraphs with ease? The ASVAB wants to know. And while it might feel like it's grilling you for answers, its real purpose is to match your skills with roles where you'll thrive.

The test is broken down into several sections, each focusing on a specific set of skills. There's Arithmetic Reasoning (AR), Mathematics Knowledge (MK), Word Knowledge (WK), Paragraph Comprehension (PC), General Science (GS), Electronics Information (EI), Auto and Shop Information (AS), Mechanical Comprehension (MC), and Assembling Objects (AO). Whew, that's a mouthful. And yes, it's a lot - but we're going to tackle each one, one step at a time.

Now, let's talk scores. You'll hear a lot of terms thrown around - AFQT score, line scores, composite scores. It's easy to feel like you're decoding some ancient military cipher. But here's the deal: your AFQT score (Armed Forces Qualification Test score) is the big one. It's the number that determines if you can enlist in the military at all. It's calculated from four key sections: Arithmetic Reasoning, Mathematics Knowledge, Word Knowledge, and Paragraph Comprehension. In other words, those four sections are your golden ticket. Score well there, and you're off to a good start.

But beyond the AFQT, there are your *line scores*. These are what the military uses to figure out which jobs (or MOS - Military Occupational Specialties) you're qualified for. For example, a high Mechanical Comprehension score could mean you're a perfect fit for a role working with heavy machinery. A strong Word Knowledge score might put you in an administrative or communications-focused position. The point is, every section matters, even if some feel more relevant to you than others.

A Deeper Dive into Test Sections

Let's break down the test a little more. Arithmetic Reasoning will have you tackling word problems - think percentages, ratios, and basic algebra. Mathematics Knowledge, on the other hand, is all about formulas and problem-solving. Word Knowledge is testing your vocabulary, and Paragraph Comprehension is checking how well you extract meaning from written text. Then there's General Science - everything from biology to chemistry basics. Electronics Information will make you think about circuits and resistors, while Auto and Shop Information tests your knowledge about tools and basic automotive systems. Mechanical Comprehension deals with gears, pulleys, and basic physics. Finally, Assembling Objects is all about spatial awareness - think puzzles and pattern recognition.

Each section isn't just a test; it's a snapshot of your abilities. Some might feel easy, others might feel like climbing Everest barefoot. That's normal.

Real-World Applications

Here's something most people overlook: the ASVAB isn't just for military placement. The skills it measures - critical thinking, problem-solving, and comprehension - are universally valued. Employers in industries like engineering, IT, and logistics often see ASVAB scores as a bonus on resumes. So, even if your future plans don't involve military boots and camouflage, a strong ASVAB performance still holds weight.

Study Smarter, Not Harder

Look, preparing for the ASVAB isn't about cramming. It's about targeted practice. Take diagnostic tests to pinpoint your weak areas. Set up a study schedule and stick to it, even if it's just 30 minutes a day. Use flashcards, practice problems, and online resources. And for the love of all things good, don't ignore your weak points - lean into them. Struggling with math? Double down. Vocabulary giving you headaches? Spend time reading.

Test Day Strategies

On the big day, get enough sleep. Eat breakfast (seriously, don't skip it). Arrive early, and stay calm. The ASVAB isn't a monster - it's just a series of questions. Take them one at a time, pace yourself, and don't panic if you hit a tricky one.

And yes, calculators are a no-go. If math isn't your strong suit, start brushing up now with long division, fractions, and percentages.

Final Thoughts

The ASVAB isn't the endgame - it's the starting line. Whether you're headed for cybersecurity, aviation, mechanics, or administration, this test is step one. So breathe, prepare, and know that you've got this.

Now, let's dive into the first section and start breaking it all down piece by piece. Ready? Let's go.

Alright, let's cut straight to the chase. You've got this massive test looming over you, and it feels like someone just handed you a map written in a foreign language. The ASVAB isn't just any old standardized test – it's the gatekeeper to your military future, and, honestly, it's a pretty big deal. But before we dive into strategies, practice questions, and tips that'll make your brain sweat, we need to start with the basics.

First off, what *is* the ASVAB? The Armed Services Vocational Aptitude Battery isn't just a test; it's a multi-aptitude assessment designed to figure out what you're naturally good at. Are you a math whiz? Do you have a knack for mechanics? Can you decipher complex paragraphs with ease? The ASVAB wants to know. And while it might feel like it's grilling you for answers, its real purpose is to match your skills with roles where you'll thrive.

The test is broken down into several sections, each focusing on a specific set of skills. There's Arithmetic Reasoning (AR), Mathematics Knowledge (MK), Word Knowledge (WK), Paragraph Comprehension (PC), General Science (GS), Electronics Information (EI), Auto and Shop Information (AS), Mechanical Comprehension (MC), and Assembling Objects (AO). Whew, that's a mouthful. And yes, it's a lot – but we're going to tackle each one, one step at a time.

Now, let's talk scores. You'll hear a lot of terms thrown around – AFQT score, line scores, composite scores. It's easy to feel like you're decoding some ancient military cipher. But here's the deal: your AFQT score (Armed Forces Qualification Test score) is the big one. It's the number that determines if you can enlist in the military at all. It's calculated from four key sections: Arithmetic Reasoning, Mathematics Knowledge, Word Knowledge, and Paragraph Comprehension. In other words, those four sections are your golden ticket. Score well there, and you're off to a good start.

But beyond the AFQT, there are your *line scores*. These are what the military uses to figure out which jobs (or MOS - Military Occupational Specialties) you're qualified for. For example, a high Mechanical Comprehension score could mean you're a perfect fit for a role working with heavy machinery. A strong Word Knowledge score might put you in an administrative or communications-focused position. The point is, every section matters, even if some feel more relevant to you than others.

So, how do you prepare for a test like this? For starters, you need to get real about where you're at. Are you a math genius but struggle with vocabulary? Do science concepts make your head spin while you ace anything mechanical? Self-awareness is your first step. And yes, that means taking a practice test. I know, I know - practice tests are about as much fun as watching paint dry. But trust me, you need to know where your strengths and weaknesses are before you start tackling study sessions.

Oh, and let's clear something up right now: studying for the ASVAB isn't cramming. This isn't your high school history final where you could memorize a stack of flashcards the night before and skate by. The ASVAB measures skills and aptitudes you've been building your entire life. So while studying helps - and it *really* helps - it's not about stuffing random facts into your brain. It's about sharpening the tools you already have.

You'll also want to understand the logistics of test day. Most people take the ASVAB at a Military Entrance Processing Station (MEPS) or a Military Entrance Test (MET) site. The test is typically computer-based (called the CAT-ASVAB) but can also be taken on paper at certain locations. The CAT-ASVAB is adaptive, meaning the difficulty of the questions changes based on how you're answering. Get one right, and the next might be harder. Miss one, and it might ease up. It's like the test is sizing you up in real time.

And let's not forget about time management. Each section of the ASVAB has its own time limit, and while some sections will fly by, others might leave you staring at the clock like it's your mortal enemy. Practice pacing yourself. You don't need to be a speed demon, but you also can't spend ten minutes agonizing over one math problem.

Speaking of math problems, let's get one thing straight: calculators are not allowed. Yep, you heard me. You're going to be doing arithmetic the old-school way, with scratch paper and a pencil. So if your math skills are a little rusty, now's the time to start brushing up.

But here's the good news: the ASVAB isn't trying to trip you up. It's not some sadistic riddle meant to make you question your life choices. It's a straightforward assessment. If you prepare, stay calm, and give it your best shot, you'll do just fine.

So, take a deep breath and remember this: the ASVAB isn't the finish line. It's just the starting point. Whether you're dreaming of a high-tech job in cybersecurity, a hands-on role as a mechanic, or something administrative behind the scenes, this test is your first step toward making it happen.

Alright, now that we've covered the basics, let's roll up our sleeves and start tackling these sections one by one. Ready? Let's do this.

Chapter 2: Arithmetic Reasoning – Cracking the Code of Word Problems

Alright, let's face it: arithmetic reasoning doesn't exactly sound like the most thrilling thing in the world. It's not skydiving or winning the lottery. But here's the thing - this section of the ASVAB is a big deal, and it's all about real-world math. This isn't abstract algebra where X equals some cosmic mystery. This is the math you actually *use* in life. Balancing budgets, calculating discounts, figuring out how many boxes of pizza you need for your friends - this is the territory we're in.

So, what exactly is Arithmetic Reasoning (AR) testing? Simply put, it's your ability to solve math word problems. These questions present a scenario, often something semi-relatable like figuring out how many miles a car can drive on a certain amount of gas or how much carpeting is needed for a living room. Your job? Translate those words into numbers and operations, do the math, and arrive at an answer that doesn't make your math teacher weep.

Let's be honest, though: word problems have a reputation. They can be tricky. They love sneaking in irrelevant details just to mess with you. You might get a question that talks about five different numbers, three random objects, and a giraffe for no apparent reason - and only one tiny piece of that puzzle actually matters. That's why the key to success in this section is learning how to filter out the noise and focus on the actual question being asked.

Breaking Down the Problem

Every arithmetic reasoning problem follows a pattern. First, there's the *setup*. This is where the question paints you a picture - sometimes an overly colorful one. Then, there's the *question itself*, hidden somewhere in that setup. And finally, there's *the math*. Your job is to find the question, set up the math equation, and solve it correctly.

Take this classic example:

John buys 5 packs of gum, each costing $1.25. He also buys a soda for $2.50. How much money did he spend in total?

Step one: ignore all the fluff. Packs of gum? Soda? Cool story, John. What do they actually want? They want the *total cost.*

Step two: set up your math. 5 packs x $1.25 = $6.25. Add the soda: $6.25 + $2.50 = $8.75.

Step three: done. Answer: $8.75.

It's not rocket science, but it does require focus. And that's where most people get tripped up - they get lost in the details.

The Common Pitfalls

Let's talk about the classic traps the ASVAB loves to set in Arithmetic Reasoning. The first big one? *Overthinking.* People start second-guessing their math, their setup, or even their basic ability to count. Spoiler: you can count.

Another trap? *Not reading carefully.* Some questions throw in extra numbers or ask for something specific like "how much change does John get back?" instead of "how much did John spend?" One tiny word can flip the entire problem.

And then there's *panic math.* You know what I'm talking about. You're halfway through a problem, and suddenly every number starts blurring together, and you can't remember if you're adding or subtracting. Deep breath. Write it down step by step. Arithmetic isn't about speed – it's about accuracy.

Strategies That Actually Work

So how do you conquer this section without losing your mind? Here are a few golden rules:

1. **Read the problem carefully.** Seriously, don't skim.
2. **Underline or circle the important numbers and keywords.** Words like *total*, *difference*, *each*, and *per* are clues about which operation to use.
3. **Break it into smaller steps.** Solve one part at a time instead of trying to do it all in your head.
4. **Estimate when possible.** Sometimes you don't need an exact answer – just one that's close enough.
5. **Double-check your work.** If you have time, go back and make sure your math adds up.

Real-World Connections

You might be thinking, "When am I ever going to use this stuff outside the ASVAB?" And honestly? All the time. Arithmetic reasoning is budgeting your paycheck, figuring out gas mileage, splitting restaurant bills with friends, or deciding if that "50% off" sale is actually a good deal.

Military roles also rely heavily on these skills. Mechanics need to measure parts and calculate torque. Supply specialists deal with inventory counts and logistics. Even cooks in the mess hall need to scale recipes to feed hundreds of people.

Practice, Practice, Practice

The only way to get good at word problems is to practice them. A lot. But don't just do random problems - pay attention to the types of questions you struggle with. Are you tripping up on percentages? Ratios? Multi-step problems? Identify your weak spots and drill them until they're not weak anymore.

Another pro tip: talk through the problems out loud. Seriously. It might feel silly, but verbalizing the steps can help you process them better.

Final Thoughts on AR

Arithmetic reasoning might not be your favorite ASVAB section, but it's one you can absolutely master with a little effort. Stay calm, stay focused, and remember: every word problem has a logical solution. It's just a matter of finding it.

Alright, take a sip of water, stretch those brain muscles, and let's start breaking down some sample problems together. Ready? Let's do it.

Chapter 3: Mathematics Knowledge – The Formulas, the Fear, and the Fixes

Let's get one thing straight right away: math doesn't care about your feelings. It doesn't care if you're good with numbers or if you once broke out in a cold sweat during a pop quiz on algebraic equations. Math is math - it's logical, consistent, and completely indifferent to your emotional state. But here's the good news: that same consistency is also your biggest advantage. Math doesn't lie, it doesn't cheat, and if you follow the rules, it'll reward you with the right answer every single time.

The Mathematics Knowledge (MK) section of the ASVAB isn't about advanced calculus or intimidating proofs. You won't need to derive anything or solve complex integrals. Instead, this section focuses on foundational concepts - algebra, geometry, basic arithmetic, and a sprinkle of trigonometry. Essentially, it's the math you *should* have learned in high school but maybe forgot the moment you walked out of your final exam.

What's On the Test?

The MK section tests your ability to solve mathematical problems and understand mathematical principles. You'll see questions on topics like:

- Algebraic equations
- Inequalities
- Fractions and decimals
- Ratios and proportions
- Geometry basics (think angles, shapes, and area formulas)
- Basic trigonometric relationships

Now, before you groan and slam this book shut, take a breath. These aren't problems designed to trick you. They're testing whether you understand *how* math works, not if you can reinvent the Pythagorean theorem from scratch.

The Math Mindset

One of the biggest barriers people face with math isn't the math itself – it's the mindset. You know the voice: *"I'm just not a math person."* Look, nobody's born a math person. You weren't born knowing how to tie your shoes, either, but you figured it out eventually (hopefully). Math is the same way – it's a skill, not an innate talent.

Start by breaking down your fear of wrong answers. Mistakes are part of the process. Every error you make while practicing is one less mistake you'll make on the real test. Treat math problems like puzzles. Approach them with curiosity instead of dread. What's the problem asking? What tools (formulas, rules, operations) do you have to solve it?

The Formulas You'll Actually Use

Let's be real: not every math formula is worth tattooing on your forearm. But there are a handful of them that you absolutely need to know for the ASVAB. Here are a few essentials:

- **Area of a rectangle:** $A = l \times w$
- **Area of a triangle:** $A = 1/2 \times b \times h$
- **Pythagorean Theorem:** $a^2 + b^2 = c^2$
- **Slope formula:** $(y_2 - y_1) / (x_2 - x_1)$
- **Percentage formula:** $(part/whole) \times 100$

You don't need a Ph.D. in mathematics to memorize these. Write them down, stick them on your fridge, or repeat them to yourself while you brush your teeth. The more familiar they become, the less intimidating they'll feel.

Common Math Traps

If the ASVAB were a movie, the math section would have its own villain: the classic trick question. These are the ones that *look* simple but have a tiny detail hiding in plain sight. Maybe it's a unit conversion they expect you to overlook. Maybe they slipped in an extra step that wasn't immediately obvious. Here's a classic example:

If a rectangle's length is twice its width and its perimeter is 36 units, what are the rectangle's dimensions?

At first glance, it seems straightforward. But if you rush, you'll miss the relationship between the length and the width. Slow down. Write out the perimeter formula ($P = 2l + 2w$). Substitute the relationship ($l = 2w$) into the equation and solve step by step.

Rushing is the enemy here. Take your time, and double-check your setup before you dive into calculations.

Practical Tips for Studying Math

1. **Practice Every Day:** Math is like a muscle. If you don't use it, it weakens.
2. **Focus on Weak Spots:** Struggling with fractions? Drill them until they feel second nature.
3. **Use Online Resources:** There are thousands of free math tutorials, videos, and practice problems online.
4. **Write Out Every Step:** Don't try to solve complex problems in your head.
5. **Learn to Estimate:** Sometimes, an approximate answer is enough to eliminate wrong choices.

Why Math Matters Beyond the ASVAB

It's easy to dismiss math as something you'll never use in the real world. But here's the thing: math isn't just numbers - it's problem-solving. It's logic. It's understanding relationships between different pieces of information. In the military, these skills are everywhere.

Are you operating machinery? You'll need math. Calculating supplies and logistics? Math. Plotting coordinates on a map? Math again. The military runs on precision, and precision runs on math.

And even outside of the military, these skills stick with you. Whether you're budgeting, building something, or just trying to split a dinner bill fairly, math is part of daily life.

Wrapping Up Mathematics Knowledge

At the end of the day, the MK section isn't about being a math wizard - it's about being confident and prepared. The math you'll see on the ASVAB is conquerable. With some practice, a bit of patience, and maybe a little caffeine, you'll be solving equations like it's second nature.

Now, grab your pencil, take a deep breath, and let's crack open some sample problems. Because the best way to get good at math... is to do math.

Chapter 4: Word Knowledge – Cracking the Code of Vocabulary

Let's get something straight right from the start: words are sneaky little things. They can charm, confuse, clarify, or completely mislead you – all depending on how they're used. And in the ASVAB Word Knowledge section, they're not pulling any punches. This part of the test isn't about crafting Shakespearean sonnets or writing flawless essays. It's about recognizing the meaning of words, understanding their context, and – most importantly – knowing which word fits where.

So, what's the deal with the Word Knowledge (WK) section? At its core, this part of the ASVAB evaluates your vocabulary. But not just how many big, fancy words you know – it's about your ability to quickly understand what a word means in context or how it relates to other words. You'll be asked questions like:

- Which word is most similar in meaning to *obstinate*?
- What does the word *elated* most nearly mean?
- Choose the word that best fits in this sentence: *The general gave a _____ speech before the battle.*

Simple enough, right? Well, yes and no. Vocabulary isn't just about knowing definitions - it's about making connections. And sometimes, those connections are buried in tricky phrasing or surrounded by distractors that seem *almost* right.

Why Vocabulary Matters

Let's be honest: a strong vocabulary makes you sound smart. But more importantly, it helps you communicate effectively. Whether you're reading instructions, listening to commands, or writing reports, words are your tools. Misunderstanding one key term can mean the difference between following orders correctly and making a mistake.

In the military, precision is everything. Imagine misinterpreting a crucial term in a technical manual or misunderstanding an order because a single word threw you off. Word Knowledge isn't about showing off - it's about being prepared.

Common Word Knowledge Pitfalls

Here's the thing about vocabulary tests: they love to mess with you. The ASVAB likes to throw in words that *look* like other words but mean something completely different. Ever mix up *affect* and *effect*? Yeah, join the club.

Another classic trick? Synonyms that aren't *quite* right. Let's say the word is *frugal*. The choices might include:

A) Generous
  B) Cheap
  C) Economical
  D) Wealthy

The answer is C) Economical, but it's easy to pick B) Cheap if you're not careful.

Words carry connotations, and sometimes those subtle differences are what trip people up.

And then there's the "fancy word" trap. Just because an option sounds impressive doesn't mean it's correct. Don't fall for the allure of the longest or most intimidating-looking word.

Building Your Vocabulary – The Smart Way

You might be thinking, *"Okay, great. So how do I get better at this?"* Well, cramming a dictionary into your brain isn't going to cut it. Instead, focus on these strategies:

1. **Read, Read, Read:** The more you read - books, articles, instruction manuals, heck, even cereal boxes - the more words you'll encounter.
2. **Context Clues Are Your Friend:** When you see an unfamiliar word, look at the words around it. They often hold the key to understanding.
3. **Learn Roots, Prefixes, and Suffixes:** Words are built from parts. If you know that *bio-* means life or that *-ology* means the study of, you can make educated guesses.
4. **Make Flashcards (Yes, Really):** Old-school? Sure. Effective? Absolutely.
5. **Use New Words in Conversation:** If you learn a new word, use it. It'll stick better.

The Power of Context

Context is your secret weapon in the WK section. Even if you don't know a word outright, the sentence around it is often loaded with hints. Take this example:

Despite his _____ behavior, the soldier earned the respect of his peers.

Let's say the options are:

A) Erratic
   B) Courageous
   C) Timid
   D) Foolish

You might not know what *erratic* means, but words like *despite* and *earned respect* suggest a contradiction. The soldier must have been behaving in a way that wouldn't normally earn respect – but he did anyway. The answer is A) Erratic.

See how context can guide you even when the word itself feels foreign?

Avoiding Overthinking

Vocabulary questions are a breeding ground for overthinking. You might stare at a word until it stops looking like a word altogether. Or you'll convince yourself that the "obvious" choice is too obvious.

Trust your gut. Your first instinct is often right – especially if you've been studying.

Words You Should Definitely Know

While you can't predict exactly which words will show up on the ASVAB, certain words seem to love making repeat appearances. Here are a few examples:

- **Ambiguous:** Unclear or open to more than one interpretation
- **Candid:** Honest and straightforward
- **Diligent:** Hardworking and careful
- **Eloquent:** Fluent or persuasive in speaking

· **Inevitable:** Certain to happen

These words – and many like them – are worth committing to memory.

Why Word Knowledge Goes Beyond the Test

Sure, acing this section will boost your ASVAB score. But a solid vocabulary isn't just about test performance – it's about life performance. Whether you're briefing a team, writing a report, or just chatting with someone, the right words make you clearer, sharper, and more confident.

Strong communication is the glue that holds teams together. It's the difference between confusion and clarity, hesitation and decisiveness.

Reflections on Word Knowledge

The Word Knowledge section might feel like a game of mental gymnastics, but it's one you can absolutely win. Build your vocabulary steadily, pay attention to context, and don't let tricky choices trip you up.

Now, let's keep this momentum going. Up next, we're diving into Paragraph Comprehension – and trust me, it's about way more than just skimming sentences. Let's go!

Chapter 5: Paragraph Comprehension – Reading Between the Lines

Let's be honest - reading comprehension isn't exactly the flashiest skill. It's not like solving a complex math problem or assembling a high-tech gadget. But here's the thing: your ability to understand and interpret written information might just be one of the most powerful tools in your arsenal, both on the ASVAB and in life. The Paragraph Comprehension (PC) section of the ASVAB isn't here to test whether you can recite poetry or appreciate classic literature. It's here to see if you can pull useful information from a block of text - quickly and accurately.

What is Paragraph Comprehension Really About?

The PC section is pretty straightforward: you'll read short passages and answer questions about them. Sometimes you'll need to identify the main idea. Other times, you'll need to find specific details, make logical inferences, or figure out what the author is implying. It's like being a detective - but instead of chasing down suspects, you're chasing down meaning.

Let's break it down further. The questions in this section usually fall into a few common categories:

- **Main Idea:** What's the overall point of the passage?
- **Supporting Details:** What specific piece of information backs up the main idea?
- **Inference:** What can you logically conclude from what's written?
- **Vocabulary in Context:** What does a specific word or phrase mean in this passage?

None of these are trick questions, but they do require focus. You can't just skim the passage and hope the answer leaps out at you – it usually won't.

The Importance of Active Reading

Active reading is the key to dominating this section. What's active reading, you ask? It's the opposite of passively letting your eyes glide over the words while your brain plans dinner or daydreams about your weekend plans. Active reading means being engaged with the text – asking yourself questions, looking for key phrases, and staying mentally present.

A good trick? Read with a purpose. Before you even look at the answers, ask yourself: *What's the main point of this passage?* or *What detail am I supposed to be focusing on?* This keeps your brain on track.

The Art of Skimming and Scanning

Okay, I just told you not to skim. But skimming and scanning are actually two different skills, and both can help you save time if you use them correctly.

- **Skimming:** This is when you quickly read through a passage to get the *gist* of it. You're looking for the big picture – the main idea, the tone, the overall point.
- **Scanning:** This is when you look for specific details. If the question asks,

"What year did the event take place?" you can scan for numbers and dates instead of reading every single word.

The trick is knowing *when* to skim and *when* to scan. If a question asks for the main idea, skim first. If it asks for a specific fact, scan.

Common Pitfalls in Paragraph Comprehension

This section might seem straightforward, but it's littered with sneaky little traps. Here are some common ones:

- **The Distractor Answer:** This is an answer that sounds right but doesn't actually match the passage.
- **Assumption Pitfall:** Never assume anything that isn't directly supported by the text.
- **Half-True Answers:** These are answers that *start* off correct but then veer into false territory.

When in doubt, always go back to the passage. The answer is *always* in the text.

Practical Tips for Success

Here are some battle-tested strategies to help you tackle Paragraph Comprehension like a pro:

1. **Read the Questions First:** Sometimes it helps to know what you're looking for before you even start reading.
2. **Stay Focused:** If you feel your mind drifting, stop and re-read.

3. **Look for Signal Words:** Words like *however*, *therefore*, and *in conclusion* often highlight key points.

4. **Eliminate Wrong Answers:** If two answers contradict each other, they can't both be right.

5. **Trust the Passage, Not Your Instincts:** Your gut might lead you astray if you start making assumptions.

Why This Matters Beyond the Test

Paragraph comprehension isn't just about passing the ASVAB. It's about being able to understand orders, interpret manuals, and make sense of complex reports. Whether you're in logistics, engineering, or communications, you'll encounter written instructions and detailed reports all the time.

But it's not just about work. Paragraph comprehension is also about life. Ever signed a lease, read a contract, or followed assembly instructions for furniture? Yeah, you were using paragraph comprehension.

Practice Makes Proficient

Improving your reading comprehension isn't about reading more – it's about reading *better*. Start paying attention to how you read. When you're reading an article or even scrolling through social media, ask yourself questions like:

- What's the main point here?
- What evidence supports that point?
- Are there any assumptions being made?

The more you train your brain to think this way, the easier these questions will become on the ASVAB.

Staying Calm Under Pressure

Time limits are part of the challenge in this section. If you find yourself running out of time, don't panic. Prioritize the questions you feel most confident about, and don't get stuck on one tricky passage.

Take a breath. Refocus. Remember that every answer you need is right there in the text.

Finding the Meaning Between the Lines

At its core, Paragraph Comprehension is about extracting meaning from written words. It's about understanding not just *what* is being said, but *why* it's being said and *how* it all fits together.

So stay sharp, stay focused, and remember: every passage has a point. Your job is just to find it.

Let's keep the momentum going. Up next, we'll dive into General Science - where things get a little more hands-on and a lot more interesting.

Chapter 6: General Science – The World Around You, Explained

Let's get one thing straight: science isn't just for lab coats and Bunsen burners. It's not some abstract thing locked away in textbooks or confined to high school classrooms. Science is everywhere. It's in the engine of your car, the battery of your phone, and the weather forecast you checked this morning. And on the ASVAB, General Science (GS) is all about testing how well you understand the basics of how the world works.

What's on the Test?

The General Science section covers a wide range of topics, but don't worry - you're not expected to be a rocket scientist or a marine biologist. Think of it as a broad survey of the sciences, touching on the essentials from three major fields:

1. **Life Science:** Biology, ecosystems, human anatomy, and basic genetics.
2. **Physical Science:** Chemistry, physics, energy, and matter.
3. **Earth and Space Science:** Weather, geology, astronomy, and environmental science.

You might see a question asking about photosynthesis, another about the periodic table, and then one about the water cycle. The key isn't memorizing every science fact in existence - it's understanding the core concepts and being able to apply them.

Why General Science Matters

You might be thinking, *"Why does a mechanic need to know about photosynthesis?"* Fair point. But the ASVAB isn't just about fitting you neatly into one role - it's about evaluating your overall ability to learn and apply information. Science, at its heart, is about observation, problem-solving, and critical thinking - skills that are essential in *any* military role.

Take chemistry, for example. If you're working with fuel systems or explosives, understanding chemical reactions could mean the difference between success and disaster. Or consider weather patterns - pilots, navigators, and even ground troops need to understand how shifting weather can affect their missions.

Life Science Basics

Life science questions on the ASVAB usually focus on biology and the natural world. You might see questions about:

- The process of photosynthesis
- Human body systems (circulatory, respiratory, nervous)
- Ecosystem dynamics and food chains
- Basic genetics (dominant vs. recessive traits)

For example, a question might ask:

Which part of the cell is responsible for producing energy?

A) Nucleus
   B) Mitochondria
   C) Ribosome
   D) Chloroplast

The answer is B) Mitochondria. They're often called the "powerhouses of the cell" because they generate energy.

Physical Science Essentials

Physical science questions often deal with chemistry and physics. You might need to know:

- Basic principles of motion and force (Newton's Laws)
- States of matter (solid, liquid, gas)
- Chemical elements and the periodic table
- Simple energy concepts (kinetic vs. potential energy)

Here's an example question:

What happens to water at 100 degrees Celsius?

A) It freezes
   B) It evaporates
   C) It condenses
   D) It turns into ice

The answer is B) It evaporates. At 100°C, water transitions from a liquid to a gas.

Earth and Space Science Highlights

This section might include questions about:

- Layers of the Earth (crust, mantle, core)
- The water cycle
- Basic astronomy (planets, stars, moon phases)
- Weather patterns and climate zones

For example:

What layer of the atmosphere contains the ozone layer?

A) Troposphere
  B) Stratosphere
  C) Mesosphere
  D) Thermosphere

The answer is B) Stratosphere. The ozone layer, which protects us from harmful UV rays, is found there.

How to Study Smart for General Science

The trick to mastering General Science isn't memorization – it's building a solid foundation. Here are some tips to keep in mind:

1. **Understand, Don't Memorize:** Focus on the *why* and *how*, not just the facts.
2. **Focus on Key Topics:** Biology, chemistry, physics, and Earth science are the big hitters.

3. **Use Everyday Examples:** Think about how science shows up in your daily life - cooking, driving, or even taking medicine.
4. **Watch Educational Videos:** Sometimes a quick animation about photo-synthesis or Newton's Laws can make things click.
5. **Practice, Practice, Practice:** Go through sample questions and get familiar with the format.

Common Pitfalls in General Science

One of the biggest mistakes people make in this section is overthinking. Science tends to follow logical rules, so if something seems overly complicated, you might be missing a simple answer.

Another trap? Ignoring context clues. Sometimes the question itself gives away hints if you read carefully.

Lastly, don't get intimidated by big scientific words. Break them down. *Photosynthesis?* Photo = light, synthesis = to put together. Boom, it's the process plants use to turn light into food.

Why Science Skills Matter Beyond the Test

General Science might seem like a random mix of topics, but the skills you build here - critical thinking, pattern recognition, and logical reasoning - are universally useful.

In the military, these skills can help you troubleshoot technical equipment, understand environmental conditions, or make quick decisions under pres-sure. Outside the military, they help you navigate the world - whether it's understanding product labels, managing household chemicals, or simply appreciating how incredible our planet is.

A Final Word on Science

Science isn't just a subject – it's a way of thinking. It's curiosity. It's asking questions and looking for answers. The ASVAB General Science section isn't expecting you to know everything, but it *is* expecting you to stay sharp, stay focused, and rely on your reasoning skills.

So keep your head in the game, trust your instincts, and remember: science is everywhere. Now, let's keep moving. The next section is all about Electronics Information, and things are about to get a little more technical.

Chapter 7: Electronics Information – Wires, Currents, and Circuits Explained

Electronics can feel intimidating at first glance. electronics can feel intimidating. Between the symbols, formulas, and diagrams that look like they were drawn by an over-caffeinated robot, it's easy to feel like this section of the ASVAB was designed specifically to make your brain short-circuit. But here's the thing - electronics, at their core, are all about patterns, logic, and some surprisingly simple principles.

The Electronics Information (EI) section of the ASVAB isn't here to turn you into an electrical engineer overnight. It's about testing your basic understanding of electrical concepts, components, and how they all work together. Whether you're aiming for a role in avionics, communications, or any job that involves tech, this section serves as a foundation.

What's on the Test?

The EI section covers a mix of foundational principles and basic applications. You'll encounter questions on:

- **Current and Voltage:** Understanding how electricity flows and how voltage drives that flow.

- **Resistance and Ohm's Law:** The relationship between voltage, current, and resistance.
- **Circuits:** Series circuits, parallel circuits, and how current behaves in each.
- **Electronic Components:** Resistors, capacitors, transistors, diodes - you know, all the little doodads on circuit boards.
- **Power and Energy:** How electrical energy is converted into other forms of energy (like light or heat).
- **Tools and Safety Practices:** Multimeters, soldering tools, and general safety protocols when working with electronics.

At first glance, these topics might seem like a random jumble of concepts, but trust me, they're all interconnected. Electricity isn't magic - it's science. And like most sciences, it follows rules.

Current, Voltage, and Resistance – The Big Three

If there's one thing you absolutely need to wrap your head around, it's the relationship between current, voltage, and resistance. Enter Ohm's Law:

$V = I \times R$

Where:

- V is voltage (measured in volts)
- I is current (measured in amperes, or amps)
- R is resistance (measured in ohms)

This formula is like the holy grail of electronics. If you know two of these variables, you can always calculate the third. Let's break it down with a quick example:

If a circuit has a voltage of 12 volts and a resistance of 4 ohms, what's the current?

Using Ohm's Law: 12 volts ÷ 4 ohms = 3 amps

Boom. Math magic.

Circuits: Series vs. Parallel

If Ohm's Law is the foundation, circuits are the framework. You'll encounter two main types: **series circuits** and **parallel circuits**.

- **Series Circuit:** Components are arranged end-to-end. Current flows through one path. If one component fails, the whole circuit stops working – like Christmas lights when one bulb burns out.
- **Parallel Circuit:** Components are arranged side by side. Current has multiple paths to follow. If one component fails, the rest of the circuit keeps chugging along.

A common question might look like this:

In a series circuit with three resistors of 2 ohms each, what's the total resistance?

Simple - add them up: $2\Omega + 2\Omega + 2\Omega = 6\Omega$

In a parallel circuit, it gets trickier because the total resistance decreases as more resistors are added. But don't worry - we'll tackle a few examples in the practice problems.

Meet the Components

If circuits are the framework, components are the building blocks. Here are the all-stars you'll want to know:

- **Resistor:** Limits current flow. Measured in ohms.
- **Capacitor:** Stores and releases energy.
- **Transistor:** Acts like a switch or amplifier.
- **Diode:** Allows current to flow in one direction only.
- **Fuse:** A safety device that breaks the circuit if too much current flows.

You might get a question like:

Which component allows current to flow in one direction only?

Answer: **Diode.**

These components might sound complex, but their functions are pretty straightforward once you break them down.

Tools of the Trade

No electrician walks into a job empty-handed. Some common tools you might see referenced in this section include:

- **Multimeter:** Measures voltage, current, and resistance
- **Oscilloscope:** Displays electrical signals as waveforms.
- **Soldering Iron:** Joins components together.

You might get a question like:

Which tool would you use to measure electrical current?

Answer: **Multimeter.**

Power and Energy

Electrical power is measured in watts, and you'll often use this formula:

P = V × I

Where:

- P is power (watts)
- V is voltage (volts)
- I is current (amps)

If a device runs on 120 volts and draws 2 amps of current, its power consumption is: 120 × 2 = 240 watts.

Understanding this relationship helps you figure out energy consumption and efficiency – critical knowledge for anyone working with electrical systems.

Study Tips for Electronics Information

1. **Get Hands-On:** If you can, tinker with basic circuits. Build something simple, like an LED light circuit.
2. **Memorize Key Formulas:** Ohm's Law and power calculations are non-negotiable.
3. **Learn the Symbols:** Electrical diagrams are full of symbols for components. Get familiar with them.
4. **Use Visual Aids:** Diagrams and flowcharts can make complex ideas click.
5. **Practice Problems:** The more you solve, the more confident you'll feel.

Why Electronics Matter

You might not become an electrician after taking the ASVAB, but electronics knowledge is essential across countless military roles. Whether you're maintaining communication systems, troubleshooting radar equipment, or working on vehicle electrical systems, understanding the basics will save time, money, and - most importantly - prevent accidents.

Outside the military, this knowledge is just as valuable. From fixing your own gadgets to understanding why your phone charger overheats, electronics is everywhere.

Final Thoughts on Electronics

Electronics isn't about memorizing random facts - it's about understanding systems and how they interact. Patterns, relationships, and logic are your best friends here. Break things down, follow the rules, and don't be afraid to revisit the basics if something doesn't click.

Alright, ready to spark some circuits? Let's jump into the next section and keep this momentum going.

Chapter 8: Auto and Shop Information – Nuts, Bolts, and Know-How

Engines hum, gears grind, and wrenches turn - there's something deeply satisfying about understanding how machines work. The Auto and Shop Information (AS) section of the ASVAB taps into this universal curiosity, measuring your knowledge of automotive systems, tools, and workshop practices. Whether you're someone who's been elbow-deep in car engines since middle school or you've only ever glanced under a hood with mild confusion, this chapter will help you navigate what to expect.

What's on the Test?

The Auto and Shop Information section splits into two general categories:

1. **Automotive Systems and Maintenance:** Questions about engines, transmissions, brakes, electrical systems, and routine car maintenance tasks.
2. **Workshop Tools and Practices:** Questions about hand tools, power tools, safety procedures, and standard workshop operations.

Expect questions like:

- *What's the purpose of a carburetor?*
- *Which tool is used to remove a spark plug?*
- *What safety gear is essential when operating a circular saw?*

While you don't need to be a certified mechanic to ace this section, a basic understanding of cars, tools, and common mechanical tasks will give you a major edge.

Under the Hood – Automotive Basics

Cars are essentially giant, complicated puzzles made up of smaller systems working together. The ASVAB focuses on the most critical of these systems:

- **Engines:** Internal combustion engines, engine components (cylinders, pistons, crankshafts), and fuel systems.
- **Transmissions:** Manual vs. automatic systems and how power gets from the engine to the wheels.
- **Brakes:** Disc brakes, drum brakes, and hydraulic systems
- **Electrical Systems:** Batteries, alternators, and ignition systems.
- **Cooling Systems:** Radiators, water pumps, and antifreeze.

For example: *Which part of an engine converts linear motion into rotational motion?*

Answer: **Crankshaft.**

Each component serves a specific purpose, and understanding these relationships is key to answering the test questions.

Workshop Essentials – Tools and Techniques

If the automotive section is about *what* machines do, the shop section is about *how* you interact with them. This part tests your familiarity with:

- **Hand Tools:** Wrenches, screwdrivers, pliers, and sockets.
- **Power Tools:** Drills, saws, grinders, and pneumatic tools.
- **Measurement Tools:** Micrometers, calipers, and torque wrenches.
- **Workshop Safety:** Protective gear, safe tool use, and hazard prevention.

Sample question: *Which type of saw is best for cutting curves in wood?*

Answer: **Jigsaw.**

Knowing the right tool for the job – and how to use it safely – will make this section a lot easier.

The Language of Mechanics

Mechanics have their own vocabulary, and the ASVAB loves to quiz you on it. Words like *torque*, *compression*, *viscosity*, and *lubrication* might pop up in questions, and they all have very specific meanings.

For instance: *What does oil viscosity refer to?*

Answer: **The thickness or resistance to flow of the oil.**

Understanding these terms isn't just about passing the test – it's about being able to follow instructions, interpret manuals, and communicate effectively in a mechanical environment.

Common Pitfalls in Auto and Shop

This section has its share of trick questions and common traps. Here's what to watch out for:

1. **Overthinking Common Sense Questions:** Sometimes the answer is simpler than it seems.
2. **Mixing Up Tools:** A wrench is not a ratchet, and a drill is not a driver.
3. **Forgetting Safety Basics:** Safety gear and protocols aren't just filler - they're essential knowledge.

When in doubt, go with the most logical, practical answer.

Real-World Applications

Why does this section matter? Because vehicles and tools are everywhere. In the military, auto and shop knowledge applies to roles in vehicle maintenance, equipment repair, and field operations. Mechanics ensure transport vehicles are roadworthy, machinists create and fix metal components, and technicians maintain essential machinery.

Even outside the military, these skills are valuable. Changing your own oil, repairing a leaky faucet, or assembling furniture without pulling your hair out? That's all auto and shop knowledge in action.

Study Tips for Auto and Shop Information

1. **Get Hands-On Experience:** If you can, spend time in a workshop or garage.
2. **Learn Tool Names and Functions:** Flashcards can help with this.
3. **Watch Tutorials:** YouTube is a goldmine of mechanical know-how.
4. **Understand Key Systems:** Know how engines, brakes, and transmissions

operate.

5. **Stay Curious:** If you've ever wondered how something works, look it up.

Connecting the Dots

At its core, the Auto and Shop section of the ASVAB is about problem-solving. Whether it's diagnosing why an engine isn't running or figuring out which tool will do the job right, this test measures your ability to think logically and practically.

It's also about confidence. Many people get nervous around tools and machinery because they seem complex or intimidating. But when you break them down into their components and functions, they become far less mysterious.

Why This Knowledge Sticks

One of the best things about auto and shop knowledge is that it's hands-on and immediately useful. You don't need to wait for some abstract future scenario to put it into practice. Whether it's changing a tire, fixing a leaky faucet, or safely using a power drill, these are skills you'll use for the rest of your life.

And hey, there's something undeniably cool about being the person who knows how to fix things. Whether you're under the hood of a Humvee or just helping a friend assemble their new IKEA bookshelf, these skills give you independence and confidence.

So, keep your tools sharp, your mind sharper, and your curiosity wide open. Let's roll into the next section - it's time to tackle Mechanical Comprehension.

Chapter 9: Mechanical Comprehension – Understanding How Things Move and Work

The world runs on mechanics. From the gears inside a wristwatch to the colossal turbines of a power plant, mechanical systems are everywhere. They're not just the domain of engineers and technicians – they're part of daily life, whether you realize it or not. Every time you open a door, ride a bike, or use a wrench, you're interacting with mechanical principles. The Mechanical Comprehension section of the ASVAB measures how well you understand these principles – how forces, levers, pulleys, and gears interact to make the world function.

What's on the Test?

This section dives into the core concepts of mechanics. It doesn't expect you to build a suspension bridge or design an engine from scratch, but it does want to see if you grasp the basics. Expect questions about:

- **Force and Motion:** Newton's laws, inertia, acceleration, and velocity.
- **Simple Machines:** Inclined planes, levers, pulleys, wedges, screws, and wheels.
- **Gears and Gear Ratios:** How gears transfer motion and power.
- **Fluid Dynamics:** How liquids and gases behave under pressure.

- **Energy and Work:** The relationship between force, distance, and energy.
- **Mechanical Advantage:** How machines reduce effort to perform tasks.

You might encounter questions like: *"If you double the length of a lever's effort arm, what happens to the force required to lift a load?"*

Or: *"In a system of pulleys, how does adding more pulleys affect the force needed to lift an object?"*

These aren't random trivia – they're reflections of the mechanical systems we encounter every day.

The Basics of Force and Motion

At the heart of mechanics are Newton's three laws of motion, and yes, they still apply even if you slept through physics class. Here's the gist:

1. **First Law (Inertia):** An object at rest stays at rest, and an object in motion stays in motion unless acted on by an external force.
2. **Second Law (F = ma):** Force equals mass times acceleration.
3. **Third Law:** For every action, there's an equal and opposite reaction.

For example: *"If you push a 10-kilogram object with a force of 20 Newtons, what's its acceleration?"*

Using Newton's second law: Acceleration = Force ÷ Mass = 20 N ÷ 10 kg = 2 m/s^2

These principles explain everything from rocket launches to why you slide backward when a bus suddenly accelerates.

Simple Machines – Small Tools, Big Impact

Simple machines are the unsung heroes of mechanical systems. These devices might look basic, but they amplify force and make heavy tasks manageable.

- **Levers:** A seesaw or a crowbar.
- **Pulleys:** Hoisting a flag up a pole.
- **Inclined Planes:** A ramp for loading heavy objects.
- **Wedges:** An axe splitting wood.
- **Screws:** A car jack lifting a vehicle.
- **Wheels and Axles:** A doorknob or a car tire.

The ASVAB might ask something like: *"Which type of simple machine is used in a screw jack?"*

Answer: **Screw.**

Understanding these tools isn't about memorization - it's about recognizing their everyday applications.

Gears and Ratios – Turning Power Into Precision

Gears are everywhere: clocks, bicycles, car transmissions. They're mechanical multitaskers, transferring energy and altering force and speed.

A common ASVAB question might be: *"If a large gear with 40 teeth drives a smaller gear with 10 teeth, what happens to the speed of the smaller gear?"*

Answer: The smaller gear spins four times faster.

Gear ratios aren't just math - they're about understanding how systems balance speed and power.

Fluid Dynamics – Moving Air and Water

Fluids - both liquids and gases - follow their own rules. This section often touches on:

- **Pressure and Flow:** Why water flows faster through a narrow pipe.
- **Buoyancy:** Why boats float and rocks sink.
- **Bernoulli's Principle:** Why airplanes stay in the sky.

For instance: *"What happens to water pressure as depth increases?"*

Answer: It increases.

These principles explain not only why dams are built thicker at the bottom but also why airplanes have wings shaped the way they do.

Work, Energy, and Mechanical Advantage

Work happens when force moves an object over a distance, and energy is what makes that work possible. The formula is simple:

Work = Force × Distance

Mechanical advantage, on the other hand, describes how machines reduce the effort needed to perform a task. For example, a pulley system might allow you to lift a 200-pound object by applying just 50 pounds of force.

The ASVAB might ask: *"If a lever has a mechanical advantage of 4, how much force is needed to lift a 400-pound load?"*

Answer: **100 pounds.**

Study Tips for Mechanical Comprehension

1. **Understand the Concepts, Not Just the Formulas:** Know *why* force, energy, and motion behave the way they do.
2. **Use Real-World Examples:** Think of tools, machines, or even playground equipment.
3. **Practice Diagrams:** Mechanical systems often come with illustrations. Learn to interpret them.
4. **Break Problems Down:** Take it one step at a time.
5. **Stay Calm Under Pressure:** Mechanical problems are puzzles - approach them logically.

Why Mechanical Knowledge Matters

Whether you're maintaining heavy machinery, working with aviation equipment, or troubleshooting hydraulics, mechanical comprehension is foundational. It's not just about knowing facts - it's about solving problems.

Outside the military, mechanical knowledge pops up constantly. Changing a tire, assembling furniture, or fixing a broken hinge - it's all applied mechanics.

Seeing the Bigger Picture

At the end of the day, mechanical comprehension isn't about memorizing obscure facts. It's about understanding systems, forces, and movement. It's about seeing how small components interact to create bigger results.

When you strip away the numbers, formulas, and technical jargon, mechanics are just common sense in action. Every lever, every gear, every pulley is a solution to a problem. And once you start seeing the patterns, the world of mechanics feels less like a mystery and more like a toolkit.

Alright, let's keep this momentum going. The next section is all about Assembling Objects – and trust me, it's not just about puzzles.

Chapter 10: Assembling Objects – Putting the Pieces Together

Spatial reasoning isn't just about solving puzzles or winning at Tetris - it's a fundamental skill that helps you make sense of the world. Whether you're assembling a piece of IKEA furniture, interpreting a blueprint, or visualizing how gears fit together in an engine, your ability to mentally manipulate shapes and objects is incredibly valuable. The ASVAB's Assembling Objects (AO) section measures this exact skill: your knack for seeing how pieces fit, align, and interact.

What's on the Test?

The Assembling Objects section tests your ability to visualize spatial relationships and predict how different parts come together. You'll encounter questions that involve:

- **Shape Matching:** Identifying which shape fits into a given space.
- **Pattern Assembly:** Visualizing how separate pieces combine into a whole.
- **Object Orientation:** Determining how an object looks from a different angle.
- **Spatial Sequences:** Figuring out the next step in a pattern or series.

These questions aren't about memorization - they're about perception, visualization, and mental agility.

For example, you might see a question that shows a set of shapes and asks: *"Which of the following options correctly represents how these pieces fit together?"*

Or: *"If you rotate this object 90 degrees clockwise, what will it look like?"*

The answers rely on your ability to mentally move, flip, and align objects in your head.

Why Spatial Skills Matter

At first glance, the AO section might feel like a random assortment of puzzles. But spatial reasoning plays a critical role in many real-world applications. Think about roles in engineering, mechanics, construction, or aviation. These fields rely heavily on your ability to interpret blueprints, visualize designs, and understand how parts fit together.

Even outside specialized careers, spatial skills are surprisingly universal. Whether you're packing a moving truck, organizing your kitchen cabinets, or figuring out how to wedge a couch through a narrow doorway, you're tapping into spatial reasoning.

Shape Matching – Recognizing What Fits

One of the most common question types in this section involves identifying how shapes fit together. You might see an incomplete diagram and be asked to select the missing piece from a set of options.

For example: *"Which of these shapes completes the puzzle?"*

To tackle these questions:

1. Focus on key angles and edges.
2. Eliminate options that clearly don't match.
3. Rotate and flip the shapes mentally until they align.

It's less about speed and more about accuracy. Don't rush - spend a moment studying the relationships between the pieces.

Pattern Assembly – Building the Whole Picture

Pattern assembly questions test your ability to visualize how fragmented pieces come together. Think of it like piecing together a jigsaw puzzle without the picture on the box.

These questions often require you to:

- Identify matching edges.
- Predict how shapes will align.
- Visualize the final assembled object.

A quick tip: start with the most distinct feature. Is there a unique corner, curve, or edge that stands out? Use it as your anchor.

Object Orientation – Changing Perspectives

Rotation and orientation questions challenge you to view objects from different angles. You might see a 3D shape and be asked: *"What will this object look like if rotated 180 degrees?"*

To approach these questions:

1. Break the object into smaller reference points - corners, edges, or patterns.
2. Mentally "turn" the object in your head.
3. Match the result with the given options.

Practice makes this easier over time, and even small improvements can drastically boost your score.

Spatial Sequences – What Comes Next?

These questions show a series of shapes or objects arranged in a sequence. Your task is to predict the next step.

It could involve:

- Identifying a repeating pattern.
- Spotting gradual changes in shape, size, or orientation.
- Recognizing symmetrical or rotation patterns.

The key here is observation. Patterns often hide in plain sight, and once you spot the logic, the answer becomes obvious.

Tips for Mastering Assembling Objects

1. **Practice Visualization:** Close your eyes and try to mentally rotate or flip simple shapes.
2. **Start with the Edges:** In matching or assembly questions, corners and edges often hold the most clues.
3. **Use Your Finger (If Allowed):** Tracing shapes or patterns with your finger

can sometimes help your brain process the relationships.

4. **Look for Distinct Features:** A single unique edge, curve, or pattern can narrow your options quickly.
5. **Stay Calm:** Rushing leads to mistakes. Take a breath and focus.

Why This Section Is More Than Just Puzzles

Spatial reasoning isn't just about solving abstract puzzles - it's about practical problem-solving. Engineers use it to design structures. Mechanics rely on it to assemble engines. Architects visualize entire buildings in their minds before the first brick is laid.

In the military, spatial skills come into play in everything from plotting maps to assembling equipment under pressure. And in everyday life? Well, anyone who's ever tried to load a dishwasher efficiently knows the value of spatial reasoning.

The Brain Gym for Spatial Skills

If you're feeling a bit rusty, don't worry. Spatial reasoning is like a muscle - it gets stronger with practice. Try activities like:

- Solving jigsaw puzzles.
- Playing 3D video games.
- Building models or assembling furniture.
- Drawing objects from different angles.
- Using apps or online tools designed for spatial training.

These activities aren't just fun - they sharpen your mental toolbox.

The Big Picture

At its heart, the Assembling Objects section of the ASVAB isn't about tricking you with optical illusions or impossible puzzles. It's about testing how well you can see relationships between parts, predict outcomes, and mentally manipulate shapes.

These aren't just test-taking skills - they're life skills. Whether you're troubleshooting equipment, interpreting blueprints, or even rearranging your living room furniture, spatial reasoning helps you make smarter, faster decisions.

So take a moment, breathe, and trust your brain's ability to make sense of shapes, angles, and patterns. Every question is a chance to flex those mental muscles - and once you start seeing the connections, the pieces will fall into place.

Conclusion: Wrapping It All Together

The ASVAB isn't just a test - it's a doorway. A surprisingly dense, multi-sectioned, brain-flexing doorway, but a doorway nonetheless. You've navigated arithmetic puzzles, decoded paragraphs, matched shapes, and maybe even had a minor existential crisis over Ohm's Law. But here you are - on the other side, looking back at everything you've tackled and (hopefully) feeling a little more confident about what's ahead.

Let's take a moment to reflect on what this journey has been about. This guide wasn't just a collection of practice questions and overly detailed explanations (though there were plenty of both). It was a roadmap, a flashlight in the metaphorical cave of test prep, designed to give you clarity in a process that often feels confusing and opaque.

The Bigger Picture

The ASVAB isn't the end - it's a beginning. Whether you're dreaming of fixing aircraft engines, operating high-tech communications equipment, or coordinating logistics for a unit halfway around the world, your score on this test helps determine where you'll start. But - and this is important - it doesn't define where you'll *end up.*

Tests like the ASVAB are snapshots. They measure what you know and what you can do *right now.* They don't measure your potential for growth, your determination, or your ability to learn on the fly. And those qualities? They're often what make the difference between someone who just gets by and someone who excels.

Lessons Beyond the Questions

Every section of the ASVAB has its own flavor. Arithmetic Reasoning taught you how to break down word problems and cut through the clutter to find the numbers that mattered. Mathematics Knowledge gave you formulas and patterns to lean on. Word Knowledge reminded you that precision with language isn't just for poets and novelists - it's for anyone who wants to communicate effectively.

Paragraph Comprehension showed you how to find meaning in dense blocks of text, even when it felt like the author was actively trying to confuse you. General Science gave you a whirlwind tour of biology, chemistry, and physics, while Electronics Information showed you the logical beauty behind circuits and current.

Auto and Shop Information grounded you in the real world of tools and machinery, and Mechanical Comprehension revealed the quiet rules that govern how levers lift, pulleys pull, and gears grind. Finally, Assembling Objects gave your brain a workout in spatial reasoning, challenging you to see connections where others might only see chaos.

Each section wasn't just about answering questions - it was about training your brain to think critically, to observe carefully, and to approach problems methodically. And those are skills you'll carry with you far beyond the testing room.

Confidence is Earned

Here's the thing about confidence: it's not something you're born with. It's earned. It comes from preparation, practice, and those small moments where you realize, *"Oh, I actually understand this."* Maybe it was when you finally nailed a tricky algebra problem or when you could rattle off Ohm's Law without blinking. Maybe it was when you started seeing patterns in word problems that used to feel like riddles.

That feeling? Hold onto it. Because confidence isn't just useful in a test - it's useful in life. Whether you're facing a high-pressure situation in your military career, figuring out a complex logistical problem, or just trying to keep calm in the middle of chaos, confidence is your best ally.

The Real Takeaway

If there's one thing to take away from this guide, it's this: you're capable of more than you think. Tests have a way of making people feel boxed in, like their worth is tied to a number or a percentile rank. But numbers don't measure grit. They don't measure heart. And they definitely don't measure what you'll do when the pressure's on and the stakes are high.

What the ASVAB *does* measure, though, is your starting point. It's your map, showing you where your strengths lie and where you might need to focus a little extra effort. And that's valuable information - not just for the military, but for life in general.

Moving Forward

The military is built on systems, routines, and structures. But it's also built on people - people who show up, put in the effort, and bring their best to the table every day. Whether you're enlisting to serve your country, to learn valuable skills, or to build a future for yourself and your family, the ASVAB is just the first step.

You'll face challenges - some big, some small. There will be moments of frustration, moments of doubt, and moments where you wonder why you even signed up in the first place. But there will also be moments of triumph - when you solve a problem no one else could, when you achieve something you didn't think was possible, and when you realize just how far you've come.

Keep the Momentum Going

Studying for the ASVAB isn't just about the test itself. It's about building habits - discipline, focus, and persistence - that will serve you well in every area of your life. It's about proving to yourself that you can tackle something difficult, stick with it, and come out stronger on the other side.

You've done the work. You've read the chapters, tackled the practice problems, and (hopefully) taken a few deep breaths along the way. And whether you feel fully ready or just *mostly* ready, know this: you've already taken the hardest step. You've started.

The Road Ahead

Whatever happens next - whether you ace the test on your first try or need to go back and tackle a few weak spots - know that this is just one step in a much bigger journey. The ASVAB might open doors, but it's what you do once you walk through them that really matters.

So here's to the next chapter - whatever it looks like for you. Whether it's boot camp, advanced training, or a new role in a field you're passionate about, take everything you've learned here with you. The problem-solving skills, the persistence, and yes, even those tricky algebra formulas - they're all tools in your toolbox now.

And tools, as you've learned, are only as useful as the person holding them.

Good luck out there. Not just on the ASVAB, but on everything that comes after. You've got this.

Made in the USA
Monee, IL
18 February 2025

12548741R00039